To

From

The Ten Commandments
2012 First Printing This Edition

ISBN 978-1-61261-149-5

Written and compiled by Sophie Piper
Illustrations copyright © 2012 Angelo Ruta
This edition copyright © 2012 Lion Hudson

The moral rights of the author and illustrator
have been asserted

Originally published by
Lion Hudson plc
Wilkinson House, Jordan Hill Road,
Oxford OX2 8DR, England
www.lionhudson.com

Published in the United States and Canada by Paraclete Press, 2012.
1 3 5 7 9 10 8 6 4 2 0

Acknowledgments
All unattributed prayers are by Sophie Piper, copyright © Lion Hudson.
The prayers by Lois Rock are copyright © Lion Hudson.

Bible extracts are taken or adapted from the Good News Bible published by
the Bible Societies and HarperCollins Publishers, © American Bible Society 1994,
used with permission.

Typeset in 14/18 Throhand Regular
Printed in China January 2012 (manufacturer LH17)

The *Ten* Commandments

Sophie Piper ✣ *Angelo Ruta*

PARACLETE PRESS
Brewster, Massachusetts

Introduction

According to the Bible, the Ten Commandments were given by God to a man named Moses.

This Moses, the Bible relates, was one of the many descendants of Abraham – one of the people of Israel. They believed that they had been chosen by God to bring God's blessing to all the world.

In the time when Moses was born, it seemed impossible that they would do any such thing. Once, the people had been welcome as foreigners in Egypt; now a new king, a pharaoh, had made them slaves. They toiled to turn mud into bricks for the king's splendid building projects. Slave-drivers treated them cruelly, and they were often in fear for their own lives and the lives of their children.

Moses came to believe that God wanted him to lead his people to freedom. With God's help, he convinced the pharaoh that it was time to let his Israelite slaves go. With God's help, he led them beyond the reach of the Egyptian army and into the wilderness of Sinai, on the road to the land where they would make a new home, Canaan.

On a mountain top in Sinai, amid dark clouds and thunder, Moses wrote down the great laws as God directed.

By obeying them, Moses explained the people of Israel would really be God's people. They would show God's holiness, God's love, and God's justice to all the world.

I am the Lord your God: you shall have
no other gods but me.

The world and all that is in it belong to God;
the earth and all who live on it are his.

From Psalm 24:1

God is our God,
and God alone:
love him
with all your heart,
your soul, your strength;
and keep his laws:
from them
do not depart.

From Deuteronomy 6:4–5

Praise the Lord from heaven,
all beings of the height!
Praise him, holy angels
and golden sun so bright.

Praise him, silver moonlight,
praise him, every star!
Let your praises shine
throughout the universe so far.

Praise the Lord from earth below,
all beings of the deep!
Lightning, flash! You thunder, roar!
You ocean creatures, leap.

Praise him, hill and mountain!
Praise him, seed and tree.
Praise him, all you creatures
that run the wide world free.

Let the mighty praise him.
Let the children sing,
Men and women, young and old:
Praise your God and king.

From Psalm 148

You shall not make for yourself any idol.

"What use is an idol?

"Think of it like this: a man cuts down a tree – cedar, perhaps, or oak or cypress from the forest.

"He uses some of it as fuel. The fire keeps him warm, cooks his bread, and roasts his meat. 'What a beautiful fire,' he says... and rightly so.

"The rest of the wood he carves into an idol. He bows down to it and worships it. He prays to it and says, 'You are my god – save me!'

"Can he not see how foolish he is to bow down to a block of wood? It makes as much sense as eating the ashes of his fire."

From Isaiah 44:13–20

Though the world may turn to dust,
rags and ashes, mould and rust,
I will trust in God above
and his everlasting love.

How should a person worship the living God?

Some people say, "You should worship God here, in this way."

Others say, "No! You should worship God there, in that way."

Jesus said, "God is Spirit, and only by the power of his Spirit can people worship him as he really is."

Based on John 4:24

Let the Spirit come
like the winds that blow:
take away my doubts;
help my faith to grow.

Let the Spirit come
like a flame of gold:
warm my soul within;
make me strong and bold.

Lois Rock

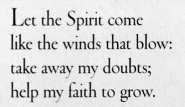

You shall not bring disgrace on the name of the Lord your God.

Do you claim to live as God wants?
Do you say you obey his laws?

Your words are not enough –
nor all your prayers and praises.

God wants you to do what is right:
to be honest and fair,
peaceable and kind,
generous and good.

Those who live as God wants
will be blessed.
They will be like a well-watered garden,
like a spring that never runs dry.

Based on Isaiah 58

I will choose the narrow path,
I will walk the straight,
Through the wide and winding world
Up to heaven's gate.

Based on Matthew 7:13–14

*Remember the sabbath
and keep it holy.*

Praise be to God on Mondays:
to the God who made day and night.

Praise be to God on Tuesdays:
to the God who made heaven and earth.

Praise be to God on Wednesdays:
to the God who made sea and land,
trees and grasses, flowers and fruit.

Praise be to God on Thursdays:
to the God who made sun and moon,
and the stars that whirl through the universe.

Praise be to God on Fridays:
to the God who made fish to fill the deep of the seas
and birds to fly high in the heavens.

Praise be to God on Saturdays:
to the God who made every kind of creature –
the great and the small, the wild and the tame;
to the God who made men and women,
girls and boys, guardians of the wide earth.

Praise be to God on Sundays:
to the God who made a day of thankfulness,
a day of rest.

Based on Genesis 1

Help me, Lord,
to be quiet and still,
to hear your voice,
to know your will.

Help me, Lord,
to sing loud and clear,
to praise your name
through all the year.

Lois Rock

O God,
It is so hard to keep my mind on my prayers. My thoughts
just run away in a butterfly meadow of daydreams.
Bring me back to the path that will lead me into your
presence.

Lois Rock

Show respect for your father and mother.

Children,
Obey your parents,
for that is the right thing to do.
God has commanded that you should
and God will bless you.

Parents,
Be worthy of your children's respect.
Take time and care to teach them well
and guide them in the way they should go.

From Paul's letter to the Ephesians, 6:1–4

Listen to your father; without him you would not exist. When your mother is old, show her your appreciation.

Truth, wisdom, learning, and good sense – these are worth paying for, but too valuable for you to sell.

A righteous person's father has good reason to be happy. You can take pride in offspring who are wise.

Make your father and mother proud of you; give your mother that happiness.

From Proverbs 23:22–25

May we learn to appreciate different points of view:

to know that the view from the hill is different from the view
   in the valley;
the view to the east is different from the view to the west;
the view in the morning is different from the view in the
   evening;
the view of a parent is different from the view of a child;
the view of a friend is different from the view of a stranger;
the view of humankind is different from the view of God.

May we all learn to see what is good, what is true,
what is worthwhile.

Lois Rock

You shall not commit murder.

Jesus said:

"You have heard that it was said, 'Love your friends, hate your enemies.' But now I tell you: love your enemies and pray for those who persecute you, so that you may become the children of your Father in heaven. For he makes his sun to shine on bad and good people alike, and gives rain to those who do good and to those who do evil.

"You must be perfect – just as your Father in heaven is perfect!"

Matthew 5:43–45, 48

Dear God,
Give us the courage to overcome anger with love.

Lois Rock

Love is giving, not taking,
mending, not breaking,
trusting, believing,
never deceiving,
patiently bearing
and faithfully sharing
each joy, every sorrow,
today and tomorrow.

Anonymous

O God,
Settle the quarrels among the nations.

May they hammer their swords into ploughs
and their spears into pruning knives...

where the tanks now roll, let there be tractors;
where the landmines explode, let trees blossom
and crops ripen.

Let there be a harvest of fruit and grain
and peace that all the world can share.

Based on Micah 4:3–5

Peaceable Jesus,
You took the loaves and fishes
and fed a multitude.

I offer you this day
a tiny gift of squabbles I refused to fight.

Please will you multiply it
among the nations of the world
so that people will turn from war
and live in peace.

You shall not commit adultery.

Husbands: be faithful to your wife;
Wives: be faithful to your husband;
Parents: raise your children to be wise;
Children: be loyal to your parents as they grow old.

Based on Proverbs 5:15–17

May I never quarrel with those nearest: and if I do, may I be quick to restore the friendship.

May I never gloat when someone who has wronged me suffers ill fortune.

When I have done or said something wrong, may I not wait to be told off, but instead be angry with myself until I have put things right.

May I respect myself.

May I always control my emotions.

May I train myself to be gentle and not allow myself to become angry.

May I love only what is good: always seek it and work to achieve it.

Eusebius (3rd century, adapted)

You shall not steal.

O God,
Fill my life with true riches:
with wisdom,
with righteousness,
with justice.

Based on Proverbs 8:12

If you have to choose between a good reputation and
great wealth, choose a good reputation.

Proverbs 22:1

If you love money, you will never be satisfied; if you long
to be rich, you will never get all you want. All you gain is
the knowledge that you are rich.

Ecclesiastes 5:10, 11

Jesus said:

"Do not store up riches for yourselves here on earth, where moths and rust destroy, and robbers break in and steal. Instead, store up riches for yourselves in heaven, where moths and rust cannot destroy, and robbers cannot break in and steal. For your heart will always be where your riches are.

Matthew 6:19–21

You shall not accuse anyone falsely.

Dear God,
Help me not to speak evil of anyone, but to be peaceful and friendly, and always to show a gentle attitude towards everyone.

From Titus 3:2

Come, my young friends, and listen to me,
and I will teach you to honor the Lord.
Would you like to enjoy life?
Do you want long life and happiness?
Then hold back from speaking evil
and from telling lies.
Turn away from evil and do good;
strive for peace with all your heart.

Psalm 34:11–14

You shall not desire anything that belongs to your neighbor.

Better to eat vegetables with people you love than to eat the finest meat where there is hate.

Proverbs 15:17

Better to eat a dry crust of bread with peace of mind than to have a banquet in a house full of trouble.

Proverbs 17:1

Dear God,
Thank you for the things I have in abundance,
to enjoy with frivolity.

Thank you for the things of which I have enough,
to enjoy thoughtfully.

Thank you for the things that I lack
that keep me trusting in your many blessings.

God feeds the birds that sing from the treetops;
God feeds the birds that wade by the sea;
God feeds the birds that dart through the meadows;
So will God take care of me?

God clothes the flowers that bloom on the hillside;
God clothes the blossom that hangs from the tree;
As God cares so much for the birds and the flowers
I know God will take care of me.

Words of Jesus

A teacher of the Law came up to Jesus and asked, "Teacher, what must I do to receive eternal life?"

Jesus answered him, "What do the Scriptures say? How do you interpret them?"

The man answered, " 'Love the Lord your God with all your heart, with all your soul, with all your strength, and with all your mind'; and 'Love your neighbor as you love yourself.' "

"You are right," Jesus replied; "do this, and you will live."

From Luke 10:25–28

Jesus was sharing a last supper with his disciples.

"I shall not be with you for much longer," he said. "And now I give you a new commandment: love one another. If you have love for one another, then everyone will know that you are my disciples."

From John 13:33–35

Words of the Apostle Paul

Paul wrote:

"The whole Law is summed up in one commandment: 'Love your neighbor as you love yourself.'

"What I say is this: let the Spirit direct your lives.

"The Spirit produces love, joy, peace, patience, kindness, goodness, faithfulness, humility, and self-control."

Paul's letter to the Galatians, 5:14, 16, 22–23

Dear God,
May I never grow tired of doing good.

From Paul's second letter to the Thessalonians, 3:13

From the Bible

The great commandments are found in the Bible, and one of the passages that refers to them says there are ten (Exodus 34, verse 28). However, the Bible does not number them. Different traditions within the Christian faith divide them slightly differently. These are the commandments as they appear in the Bible.

God spoke, and these were his words: "I am the Lord your God who brought you out of Egypt, where you were slaves.

"Worship no god but me.

"Do not make for yourselves images of anything in heaven or on earth or in the water under the earth. Do not bow down to any idol or worship it, because I am the Lord your God and I tolerate no rivals. I bring punishment on those who hate me and on their descendants down to the third and fourth generation. But I show my love to thousands of generations of those who love me and obey my laws.

"Do not use my name for evil purposes, for I, the Lord your God, will punish anyone who misuses my name.

"Observe the sabbath and keep it holy. You have six days in which to do your work, but the seventh day is a day of rest dedicated to me. On that day no one is to work – neither you, your children, your slaves, your animals, nor the foreigners who live in your country. In six days I, the Lord, made the earth, the sky, the sea, and everything in them, but on the seventh day ~ I rested. That is why I, the Lord, blessed the sabbath and made it holy.

"Respect your father and your mother, so that you may live a long time in the land that I am giving you.

"Do not commit murder.

"Do not commit adultery.

"Do not steal.

"Do not accuse anyone falsely.

"Do not desire another man's house; do not desire his wife, his slaves, his cattle, his donkeys, or anything else that he owns."

Exodus 20:1–17 and also Deuteronomy 5:1–21